*Jellicle Cats come out to-night,*
*Jellicle Cats come one come all:*
*The Jellicle Moon is shining bright—*
*Jellicles come to the Jellicle Ball.*

# CATS

## The Book of the Musical

Music by Andrew Lloyd Webber

Based on *Old Possum's Book of Practical Cats*
by T. S. Eliot

Photographs and drawings by John Napier

A Harvest/HBJ Book
**Harcourt Brace Jovanovich, Publishers**
**San Diego      New York      London**

The text comprises extracts from the lyrics, based on *Old Possum's Book of Practical Cats* by T. S. Eliot; some previously unknown or uncollected poems by him; and quotations early and late from his *Collected Poems 1909-1962*. The lyric "Memory" is by Trevor Nunn, and it incorporates lines from Eliot's "Rhapsody on a Windy Night" and other Prufrock poems. The Prologue "Jellicle Songs for Jellicle Cats" contains additional material written by Trevor Nunn and Richard Stilgoe. Assistant photographer, Cathy Blaivas

Library of Congress Cataloging in Publication Data
Main entry under title:

Cats, the book of the musical.

 1. Lloyd Webber, Andrew, 1948-    . Cats.
I. Eliot, T. S. (Thomas Stearns), 1888-1965. Old
Possum's book of practical cats.
ML410.L78C4     1983        782.81′092′4          82-48026
ISBN 0-15-615582-6   (Harvest/HBJ : pbk.)

Printed in the United States of America

E

# Contents

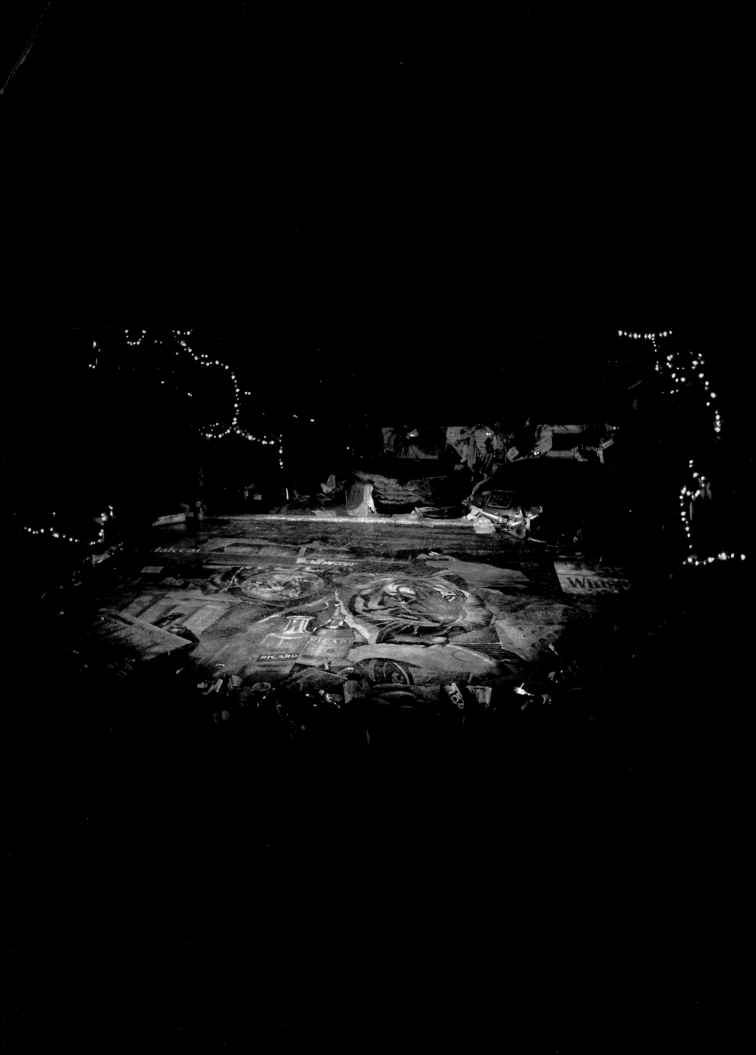

# Apropos of *Practical Cats*   by Valerie Eliot

*Photo by E. McKnight Kauffer*

T. S. ELIOT 1938

In an early poem, 'The Love Song of J. Alfred Prufrock', T. S. Eliot likened the yellow fog of St. Louis to a cat

'. . . that rubs its back upon the window-panes,
The yellow smoke that rubs its muzzle on the window-panes,
Licked its tongue into the corners of the evening,
Lingered upon the pools that stand in drains,
Let fall upon its back the soot that falls from chimneys,
Slipped by the terrace, made a sudden leap,
And seeing that it was a soft October night,
Curled once about the house, and fell asleep . . .'

He also remarked that 'The great thing about cats is that they possess two qualities to an extreme degree—dignity and comicality'.

'I am glad you have a cat', TSE wrote to his godson, Tom Faber, on 20th January 1931, 'but I do not believe it is so remarkable a cat as My cat. . . . There never was such a Lilliecat.

       ITS NAME IS
        J E L L Y L O R U M

and its one Idea is to be
              USEFUL!!

FOR Instance

IT STRAIGHTENS THE PICTURES —

IT DOES THE GRATES —

LOOKS INTO THE LARDER TO SEE
WHAT'S NEEDED —

AND INTO THE DUSTBIN TO SEE
THAT NOTHING'S WASTED —

AND YET
   IT IS SO LILLIE AND SMALL
      THAT
IT CAN SIT ON MY EAR!

(Of course I had to draw my Ear rather Bigger than it Is to get the Lilliecat onto it).

I would tell you about our Cus Cus Praps except that I can't Draw Dogs so well as Cats, Yet; but I mean to. . . .'

This was the first occasion on which Old Possum revealed himself. When Tom was four TSE suggested that all Pollicle Dogs and Jellicle Cats should be

'INVITED to Come
With a Flute & a Fife & a Fiddle & Drum
With a Fiddle, a Fife, & a Drum & a Tabor
To the Birthday Party of THOMAS ERLE FABER!'

Then there was 'a very Grand Cat . . . a Persian Prince and it is Blue because it has Blue Blood, and its name was MIRZA MURAD ALI BEG but I said that was too Big a Name for such a Small Flat, so its name is WISKUSCAT. But it is sometimes called The MUSICAL BOX because it makes a noise like singing and sometimes COCKALORUM because it Looks like one. (Have you ever seen a Cockalorum? Neither have I)'. In April 1932 Tom learnt that 'the Porpentine cat has been in bed with Ear Ache so the Pollicle Dog stopped At Home to Amuse it by making Cat's Cradles'.

TSE was always inventing suitable cat names, as he was often asked for them by friends and strangers. I remember 'Noilly Prat' (an elegant cat); 'Carbuckety' (a knock-about cat); 'Tantomile' (a witch's cat); he also liked 'Pouncival' with its *Morte d'Arthur* flavour, and 'Sillabub', a mixture of silly and Beelzebub.

Most of the poems were written between 1936 and 1938. 'I have done a new cat, modelled on the late Professor Moriarty but he doesn't seem very popular: too sophisticated perhaps . . .' TSE wrote to Frank Morley. This will surprise today's many admirers of 'Macavity'. Although he confided to Enid Faber on 8th March 1938 that 'The Railway Cat (LMS) is rather stuck', a week later the poem was finished. 'Skimbleshanks' is based on Kipling's 'The Long Trail' just as 'The Marching Song of the Pollicle Dogs' was written to the tune of 'The Elliots of Minto'. 'Grizabella the Glamour Cat' is an unpublished fragment of which only the last eight lines were written because TSE realised she was developing along the lines of Villon's 'La Belle Heaulmière' who fell on evil days and he felt it would be too sad for children.

About this time, when he was driving to the country, he and the driver began discussing their respective dogs. The chauffeur wishing to make clear that his was a mongrel said, 'He is not what you would call a consequential dog'. This so delighted TSE that he resolved to write a book of Consequential Dogs to match the Practical Cats. But, alas, it was never done. During the war when he was living with friends in Surrey he remarked of the temporary absence of a noisy pug, 'When does ". . . that fatall and perfidious Bark / Built in th' eclipse, and rigg'd with curses dark . . ." return to us?' (Milton).

Although Faber & Faber announced 'Mr. Eliot's book of *Pollicle Dogs and Jellicle Cats* in their 1936 Spring catalogue, TSE had run into difficulties over his general approach. 'The idea of the volume was to have different poems on appropriate subjects . . . recited by the Man in White Spats. . . . At the end they all go up in a balloon, self, Spats, and dogs and cats.

'Up up up past the Russell Hotel,
Up up up to the Heaviside Layer.'

Three more years, as his publisher put it, brought 'a growing perception that it would be impolite to wrap cats up with dogs' and the realisation that the book would be exclusively feline. Ralph Hodgson, the poet who bred bull-terriers, had hoped to illustrate it but at the crucial period he was house-hunting in America. He felt that 'the fun of doing it—or attempting it—is the thing, and that is only possible with my feet up on the mantelpiece, as the saying is'.

*Old Possum's Book of Practical Cats* was published in England on 5th October 1939 in an edition of 3005 copies at 3/6d with TSE's drawings on the front cover and the dust-wrapper. He was nervous about its reception. His verse play *The Family Reunion* had appeared in March and *The Idea of a Christian Society* was due in three weeks. 'It is intended for a NEW public', he informed Geoffrey Faber, 'but I am afraid cannot dispense with the old one'. He need not have worried. '*Cats* are giving general satisfaction', the Sales Manager reported shortly afterwards, while the *Manchester Guardian* said they partook 'of the infinite variety of human nature'. Today they are a minor classic and have been translated into a dozen languages.

Of the poets who have written about cats TSE most admired Christopher Smart: 'His poem about his cat is to all other poems about cats what the *Iliad* is to all other poems on war'.

P.S. Whenever he was unwell or could not sleep, TSE would recite the verses under his breath.

OP AND THE PRACTICAL CAT

WATCHING BIRDS.

# 'Up up up to the Heaviside Layer'  by Andrew Lloyd Webber

I began setting *Old Possum's Book of Practical Cats* to music late in 1977, partly because it is a book I remember with affection from my childhood and partly because I wanted to set existing verse to music. When I have written with lyricists in the past we have agreed together the dramatic structure, but for the most part the lyrics have been written to the music. So I was intrigued to see whether I could write a complete piece the other way round.

Very luckily *Old Possum* contains verses that are extremely musical; they have rhythms that are very much their own, like 'Rum Tum Tugger' or 'Old Deuteronomy' and although clearly they dictate to some degree the music that will accompany them they are frequently of irregular and exciting metre and are very challenging to a composer.

I wrote some settings in late 1977, which I began performing at the piano for friends, but I never progressed the idea seriously until after I had composed *Tell Me on a Sunday*. This was performed on BBC television in the early part of 1980, and I began to think of *Old Possum* as a possible concert anthology that could also be performed on television. With this in mind, some of my settings were performed in the summer of 1980 at the Sydmonton Festival. Valerie Eliot fortunately came to the concert and brought with her various unpublished pieces of verse by her husband. One of these was 'Grizabella the Glamour Cat'. The musical and dramatic images that this created for me made me feel that there was very much more to the project than I had realised. I immediately decided that I needed the support of another to encourage me to re-work my settings and to see if a dramatic whole could be woven from the delightful verse that I was now to be allowed to develop.

Thus in the late summer I had my first meeting with Trevor Nunn. Soon after, Mrs Eliot produced various other uncollected poems, two of which we have incorporated into *Cats* in their entirety. She also gave us a fascinating rough draft of an opening poem for what appears to have been conceived as a longer book about cats and dogs. This poem was not appropriate for the stage but it inspired us to write a lyric with the same intention of celebrating the supremacy of Jellicle cats. We have been able to include lines from the end of Eliot's draft poem which now introduce 'The Naming of Cats'. But what was most thrilling was to find a reference in one of Eliot's letters to a coherent, albeit incomplete, structure for an evening: he proposed that eventually the cats were to go 'Up up up past the Russell Hotel, up up up to the Heaviside Layer'.

Trevor Nunn, who I discovered has a taste for tackling theatrical problems that most people consider insoluble, set to work immediately with me combing Eliot's works, and we were reminded of the many references to cats in the main body of his writing. We worked on the incomplete structure and were able to incorporate some of these feline references into *Cats* without alteration. The opening poem was completed by Trevor Nunn with the aid of Richard Stilgoe, while 'Memory' was adapted from 'Rhapsody on a Windy Night'.

Of course the other very exciting opportunity that *Cats* gave me was the chance to compose dance music. This is an area of musical theatre that has always intrigued me and I was fortunate to be guided through the unfamiliar world of choreography by someone as experienced as Gillian Lynne. For the opening in New York we had the added excitement of working with American dancers and actors. Their contribution is also reflected in certain changes made to the score.

I have enjoyed *Cats* possibly more than any production on which I have worked to date. My gratitude will be undying to Valerie Eliot, without whose encouragement the musical could never have taken its present form.

# Tails of Two Cities  by Trevor Nunn

After the event we tend in the theatre to take an Olympian view of our successes and failures, and looking back through diaries and notebooks, we find there was meaning and purpose, as there is in tea-leaves. The making of *Cats* can be commemorated as many ways as there were collaborators to draw their subjective conclusions, but it seems to me that a brief record of mishap and might-have-been can only add piquancy to a volume that illustrates what finally was.

I have on occasion been tempted to believe that some of Shakespeare's plays had the unlikeliest origins; a chance remark, a broadsheet, an unrepeatable joke. I was not in the least surprised to discover that *Old Possum's Book of Practical Cats* was Eliot's book of strays—half-thoughts without a grand design; and I am not in the least abashed to admit that our musical based on T. S. Eliot's book was created haphazardly, through fervent trial and regular error.

Andrew Lloyd Webber's fascination with the poems came first. He discovered that Eliot was a lyricist as well as a poet; not only were the metres inventive, the rhyme schemes full of wit and the beat unfailingly maintained, but also the poems abounded in colloquialisms, catch phrases and choruses.

Andrew set many of the poems, gathered some friends, and at his festival at Sydmonton presented a first performance. In a sense the event was entirely in keeping with the manner in which Eliot came to write about his cats—for friends, for the children of friends, for an admiring circle, finding a huge audience only diffidently, stepping backwards into the limelight; all very English.

When I first heard the 'Sydmonton Tapes' (a shorthand phrase used repeatedly during our preparation period that always fell upon my ear as le Carré-esque) I felt sure the right thing was to recommend to Andrew that he should be thinking of a chamber theatre event, with at most five talented performers and a quintet. Certainly I found it hard to reconcile this material with dreams of creating a popular show which could dismantle class and ethnic barriers, and which would be celebratory and uplifting, the familiar fantasies of all who set out to conquer The British Musical.

Clearly the main problem was—some would say still is—the absence of a narrative. Eliot didn't write one and to be at all true to his intentions, we too would have to make do without one. I doodled many a spectral plot-line as I re-read *Alice in Wonderland*, casting Eliot's Man In White Spats—a figure he proposed should be our guide in the cat world, a sort of Debrett of the felines—as the White Rabbit, and envisioned a dream-like landscape full of improbability. Curiously, many ideas from that early stage of development have survived like ancient remains discovered intact above ground. Eventually it became clear to us that we had to find the suggestion of a narrative within or beneath the poems.

The discovery of the fragment 'Grizabella: the Glamour Cat' was probably the fulcrum moment in our planning. Here in eight lines Eliot was describing an intensely recognisable character with powerful human resonances, while introducing the themes of mortality, and the past, which occur repeatedly in the major poems. We decided that if Eliot had thought of being serious, touching, almost tragic in his presentation of a feline character, then we had to be doing a show which could contain that material, and the implications of it. Furthermore, we would have to achieve the sense of progression through themes more than incidents.

I had established with John Napier that we needed an environment rather than a set, and that we would have to find our space before we could make a start on the design. After a long search, the New London Theatre, well known as London's greatest theatrical white elephant, was measured for the task by John, beneath the baleful gaze of Producer, Composer, Director and Theatre Manager. The Choreographer danced in it a bit. Many heads were shaken and gloved hands thrust deeper into astrakhan overcoats. We would have to create a new auditorium configuration inside Sean Kenny's adaptable theatre. Not for us the tailoring of our show to a theatre; we had to be tailoring a theatre for our show.

We talked of the need to create in feline scale an alley, or a backyard. A few days later John spread a crinkled watercolour rendered on cheap paper on the floor of my office at the Aldwych. I hope he still has it. It's the equivalent of the first draft of a poem by a major writer—hundreds of changes to be made, but the thing itself, the reckless thing itself, was there.

Auditioning on an unprecedented scale (Glasgow, Manchester, Bristol, Birmingham, London) proceeded in the time-honoured American manner (low-level shots of rushing train wheels), structuring of the material made slow or rapid progress depending upon which restaurant it was being undertaken in, and the collaborators complained, as they always do, that somebody else knew more about what was happening than they did.

A cast was decided upon by a mixture of first impressions and last rounds, more cruel than *Chorus Line* could ever reveal: there is no pleasure in having the power to decide. At that level of work it's not possible to say 'she is less good than she', but only, subjectively and irrationally, 'she gets the part . . . she doesn't'.

The cast were suddenly in danger of not having a show, though they didn't know it. The owners of the New London decided that conferences only could take place there, and *Cats* wasn't a conference. The protests were many and after a suspenseful week the decision was reversed and *Cats* had another life.

Rehearsals started in Chiswick, which was only all right for Gillian Lynne who lived round the corner. However, since she was working harder than anybody else the arrangement was indisputable. I cannot resist turning aside here to pay tribute to this indomitable and inimitable choreographer/director/colleague/friend. And while aside, I am tempted to remark that directing hasn't necessarily got anything to do with telling people where they stand (neither necessarily has choreography). I mention this because critics in print have said, since the show is danced from beginning to end, that they were unclear about the role of the director. It was certainly the most unusual role I have ever undertaken, but among other things it involved writing and structuring material, conducting improvisations, delineating character, finding and communicating textual meaning and marrying the text with physical expression, pacing and phrasing the various sections of the show, arbitrating and adjudicating, connecting the many collaborators together by attempting to describe the intention of the whole, and carrying the can.

Soon there were no longer some dancers, some singers and some actors, but a group of performers probing a mystery, equally unfamiliar with the demands being made and equally prepared (that most vital of all rehearsal conditions) to be foolish in each other's eyes. From thence mysteriously flows mutual respect.

Every group has a natural leader. We lost ours unexpectedly and tragically in the third week of our work. Judi Dench was walking across an almost empty rehearsal room when she collapsed, crying out as if felled by a blow. As friends rushed to her assistance she spoke words that chilled the hearers. 'Who kicked me?' The possibility of a snapped Achilles tendon passed through many minds at that moment and by late evening Judi, who could only move if carried, knew the worst.

She could be back with us encased in plaster just before our preview performances were scheduled to begin. In the meantime she would be in hospital, recuperating from an emergency operation.

When nearly three weeks later Judi joined me in a deserted theatre in the Haymarket where we had been rehearsing, she could hardly move and she was as vulnerable as only the truly ill can be. The theatre creaked, ghosts walked and she sang her songs into the darkness of the empty auditorium for the only time. Two days later, when she came determined to rejoin the show as scheduled, she lost her balance in a flurry of crutches and pitched off an entrance ramp into rows of ungiving seats and hurt herself worse than before. Her bravery was not lost on a company who could build on her example even if they now had to face the loss of her genius.

The theatre thrives on myths, exaggerations, miracles. Elaine Paige, more out of a sense of Andrew Lloyd Webber's need than anything, generously agreed to take over Grizabella. Pursued by journalists and cameramen, we rehearsed for two days in littered rooms with rickety furniture and naked light bulbs. Grizabella rooms. Ah, the glamour of the theatre. Crisis is a great leveller. An already unified and committed group were galvanised to require yet more of themselves. Our first preview took off. The adrenalin raced in the company and audience alike. Elaine got through. The cheers rang out. Detailed work could now begin.

It shouldn't end for a long time to come. Improving is the only way to stand still in the theatre; everything else is going backwards. We will do the show in different spaces, in different towns in different lands. We will know precisely where to begin next time, precisely what to say and how to say it, precisely what to avoid and what to master. But nothing will compare with the memory of the ecstatic strain and the grim joy of the first time we made *Cats*.

Tape running. What would you say are the differences between theatre in New York and theatre in London?

I was asked that a hundred times during the *Cats* rehearsal in New York but somehow what I said never got into print. So here at last is the answer an anxious world has been waiting for.

Surprisingly little I would say if we are discussing working conditions or the expectation of talent from an original cast— there is nothing that cannot be achieved in any field of theatrical expression, with equal success on either side of the Atlantic, contemporary or classical, legitimate or popular, musical or straight.

In my view there is no truth in the generalisation that the English artist cannot do musicals and that his American brothers and sisters cannot handle language. It is true that a much smaller part of English theatre training is devoted to musical work, and this should be remedied instantly and urgently; and it is true that American performers are not frequently *asked* by American dramatists to have a heightened sense of language, which is a shameful wastage of resources, since most American actors I have worked with can quarter a thought and double an entendre with the best of them back in the Old Country.

But there are differences. In New York the commercial theatre, dominated by the theatre-owning organisations and the producers, is the sole form of theatre that reaches a large public, and therefore taste, judgement, potential risk and permissible innovation are answerable to, even one might say formed by, the box office. In London the scene is dominated by government-subsidised theatre, and the dwindling commercial sector takes in much of its product from national and regional subsidised theatre companies. Therefore the London theatre is fundamentally more experimental and less traditional than the Broadway stage, and in something of a chicken-and-egg situation, the London theatre enjoys a wide coverage in a host of newspapers genuinely interested in the theatre as an art, and prepared to give interesting developments the benefit of the doubt. In New York there is only one serious taste-forming newspaper (highly conscious of and jealous of its power) which *is* interested in the art form but is *more* interested in delivering the judgement of success or failure, up or down, like a Roman Emperor's thumb.

A theatre business that has only smash or flop categories is problematic for investors, because if the critical judgements of journalists go against, there is no management skill or expression of faith that can alter the doom of the stricken show. So not surprisingly, nobody wants to back a high-risk enterprise; if it had been necessary to originate *Cats* in America, it might not have got off the ground.

Once *Cats* had opened in London, the wisdom and daring of many New York managements became apparent in offers received from various producers, who were agreed that the streets of New York were paved with gold; but nobody talked wisdom and daring so generously as Bernie Jacobs and Gerry Schoenfeld of the Shubert Organisation. This Yin and Yang combination, two inscrutable but opposite faces representing the unknowable, must be formidable enemies, but it was our pleasure to encounter them as quietly supportive, affable enthusiasts who had yet to discover that the word No had entered the dictionary and was available for official usage. They stuck to Yes, and if in the end time decrees that they were right not to interfere or complain, then posterity has a right to know that whatever hysteria it cost them, they kept it out of the theatre.

From the first we were given everything. Two thousand artists to audition, for instance. Meeting two thousand people with a view to getting to know them is both hard and exhilarating work. So often this person who sings flat or can't manage the dance combination turns out to be the one who has founded a children's theatre, or fought cancer of the throat, or knew J. M. Barrie, or tells you the story you wake up laughing about for weeks to come; so often that perfectly beautiful girl turns out to be hard-centred or can't laugh, or doesn't listen. What an infuriating species we are, that imperfection should be so very attractive and perfect accomplishment alienating. Americans are very good at meeting people. At auditions in England you often have to dig out what is inside like an escargot on a pin; in America it's more like soft-shelled crabs—everything is there on the plate to be eaten whole.

I had been secretly concerned that Eliot's words might sound less innocent when expressed in American accents, but this was an unnecessary fear. I realised by the end of the first day of auditions that I wanted to do an American show, not an English imitation, and therefore all the green-card-carrying expatriate Londoners in New York were going to stand much less chance of being involved. There are certain New York actors who have developed the specialist skill of speaking Oxford English, which they demonstrate by auditioning with speeches from Shakespeare's plays, spoken in a grand manner. I started to understand just how Americans must feel when they see us English playing Kaufman & Hart or O'Neill. It's not that the accents are inaccurate, it's just that the experience isn't real; imitation goods.

Personality is quite clearly as important an ingredient in *Cats* as skill. Personality and eccentricity. The chosen actors have to be able to beam their personalities through oddly shaped wigs and highly coloured make-ups and unusual physical behavior, and so their characters in performance are almost bound to be derived from constituents of their real natures. So to find out more about the real natures of the performers, it was necessary to improvise.

The improvisations lasted for many days over the first two weeks of rehearsal. Everybody played ball. Everybody was honest and serious and analytical. I kept waiting for the classic English reaction that such work is a waste of time—and it never came. Perhaps I wish I had been opposed because fighting for your life is more exhilarating than expounding the Talmud—but I wasn't opposed, and the work was happy and fascinating, and on several occasions we became enraptured.

Occasionally I became conscious of the irony that a group of incredibly fit, exquisitely muscled and co-ordinated performers were subjecting themselves to the instructions of a sedentary middle-aged specimen fast running to seed (before any of my collaborators get worried I am referring to myself). But then I would be encouraged by the experience of attending the sessions of our musical supremo, Stanley Labowski. Looking like a Rubens cherub in retirement, Stanley gives you that feeling that each rehearsal is going to be imbued with the spirit of Christmas, until somebody transgresses, when biological metamorphosis occurs. Suddenly ogreish and demonic, he terrifies the necessary results out of the palpitating throats of his subjects, caught in the glare of his rampant perfectionism. However, there is one thing Stanley Labowski cannot do: sing. His voice could smash Tiffany chandeliers at thirty paces. While demonstrating harmonies for the assembled company his face expresses the kind of relaxed delight you would associate with someone having a bullet removed from the thigh without anaesthetic or even a tot of brandy. It is a mystery appropriate to the artistic process that Stanley produces in others singing that is sonorously beautiful when his own voice makes frogs wince. It was a constant delight to observe and collaborate with somebody who is the best.

Our greatest unease proceeded from the greatest unknown; what would happen to the concept of our environmental piece in an auditorium, albeit adapted, based on a proscenium configuration? The first moment of being on a set can make the ingredients of a show fall apart. Sometimes, perceptibly and instantly, the first encounter with the stage can make everything fall together. Company and crew alike seem to know that what they have been working at for weeks separately now makes complete sense, and this knowledge, which I have often but not always encountered, produces an energy which in itself diminishes problems and creates an appetite for solutions. Well, energy flowed. Everybody plugged in.

*Cats* sets out to transport its audience to a world in which plot and conventional character development are rendered unnecessary by the experience of a fantasy without human circumscriptions. All fine and dandy until the hydraulic ramp gets stuck or a colour changer develops a death rattle, or the speakers go into feedback or a million and one other devices don't deliver. The potential for technical shambles in every minute of *Cats* is awesome, and the triumph of every department over their difficulties leads me to yearn for a roll call of everyone.

After the first run-through onstage we all cried together. Theatre is a totally emotional, some would say childishly emotional, business, but these moments of release and of feeling for each other are not to be dismissed, still less despised. Tears of relief and need constitute incontrovertible evidence of what people have risked in a rehearsal or performance, and the only theatre the public wants to know about (though they probably don't and shouldn't realise it) is the theatre that takes everything you are and everything you have to get it there, and keep it there. In America. In England. Everywhere.

So, a small group of people late at night in a darkened theatre, unable to say much, were nearly ready to expose themselves to those peculiar conditions of judgement that exist in New York and New York alone. Thumbs up. Thumbs down. Life or death. If any member of that critical fraternity were ever to feel or understand the well-spring of those tears I have tried to describe, he would see how destructive and undignified it is that caprice should govern the lives and livelihoods of artists. I am not squeezing sour grapes. *Cats* was given its life—many have predicted its nine lives—so my regret does not proceed from personal hurt. It is, in a technological age, my regret that New York could be destroying the conditions for the achievement of what it does best. And all because of a gesture from an Emperor who has no clothes.

# The choreographing of *Cats*  by Gillian Lynne

The choreographing of *Cats* is a difficult matter, it isn't just one of your everyday games. To borrow from the words of one of T. S. Eliot's marvellous poems seems the most apt way to describe my task in staging the songs and dances for *Cats*. Staging, such a seemingly all-purpose word, is taken to mean many things to many men. In my case what you see is what I begat. The process towards this birth meant certain limitations and peculiarities for my choreography (and staging) as one of its duties was to tell clearly the story of each song and not interpret it at will, because the book of the show must live within the songs and dances. Sometimes I thought my mind would burst with the pressure of the invention needed in two and a half hours of staging. The range necessary to satisfy the eye and the mind yet remain true to the titled characters had to be conjured from my past and future, and not be swayed by my ever-present nightmares. I wanted to use known and accepted dance forms in a different way; as it were putting a feline wash over them, and adapting them to a style and energy we could call our own. This meant vigorous exercises of an unusual nature, leading eventually to total freedom of what we could attempt physically. Having observed that cats are at once aloof, hypersensual, cold, warm, completely elastic and very mysterious, we found the goals we set ourselves to be physically daunting in their attempt to translate T. S. Eliot's words in an exciting, theatrical, witty, yet feline way.

I fell in love with Andrew's music the minute I heard it, and building the numbers with him, where the music needed extending to allow more dance, was hard and thrilling work. Sometimes I could not always explain what I wanted convincingly enough and then I and my little skeleton crew would dance my ideas flat out for him, trying often to look like twenty-five people. A choreographer working out the numbers for a new musical needs a skeleton crew just as a writer needs pen and ink. This little band usually consists of one's assistant, a boy and a girl dancer, the dance captain (male or female) who will then remain and take care of the show, and of course a brilliant and creative pianist. It is meticulous, nerve-wracking (will the ideas come up out of the blue?) and tiring work, mentally and physically, for this is the time when all the movement styles for each character have to be discovered, and many of the ideas for the staging and graph of each number start to be built in. I was lucky with the original London production of *Cats*; my crew were so sympathetic, patient and tireless. Lindsay Dolan, my assistant, and Finola Hughes and John Thornton, who were in the show, put up with my endless probings, frustrations, despair, breakthroughs, joy and long, long hours of work, and I shall be grateful to them always. Equally I struck lucky with my American crew, Bonnie Walker, René Cebellos and Tim Scott, whose support and dynamism were an inspiration. Joanne Robinson, who looked after the London *Cats* became my right arm on the American production; she is an indefatigable friend as well as a brilliant assistant.

Creating the Jellicle Ball was the hardest and most exciting task of all. Firstly the poem 'The Song of the Jellicles' places such an intriguing set of images in the mind, secondly the Ball is pivotal to our show, and we knew in the beginning that if we were to achieve our aim of producing England's first dance musical we had to succeed there or die. I knew I had to extend T. S. Eliot's beautiful poem and find a dance poem that carried on the ideas he suggested, to become a piece of exciting theatre whilst showing the cats at the height of their passion, dancing their most private, energetic and anarchic rituals. The day when my crew and I danced the whole thing for Andrew and Trevor, playing all the parts, trying to show the total excitement and mystery we were hoping to create, indicating where the acrobatic tricks would come (we couldn't quite manage those!) and when eventually they saw what I was after and agreed to it was an incredibly tense and rewarding occasion and worth every bit of the sweat and exhaustion that inevitably followed. John Napier's and Trevor Nunn's brilliant conception of the world in which we were to make *Cats* come alive was full of such exciting possibilities and also some difficulties. Dancing in the round, which was the shape of our London auditorium, can sometimes create havoc in the push and thrust of section, as you have to turn the corner at the end of it just as the climax is reached. Also, as we have no wings as such everyone has to be choreographed for every minute—you can't happily reassemble them in the wings for their next leap-ons. On the other hand the immediacy of the space means the audience can feel the energy of the performers and become part of it. At the Winter Garden John created another phantasmagorical world, wonderful to explore but demanding different textures from the staging. The thrust stage makes energy excitingly apparent, but it follows that the shadowy moments where our cats must be remote, wary and introspective are harder to achieve.

Making a worthy attempt at the exotic theatre of Growltiger's dreams of the Siamese, building a savage and believable cat fight for Macavity, trying to make the cockroaches succeed in a beetles' tattoo that might have echoes of Busby Berkeley, finding dance characters for the Tugger and the Pekes and Pollicles, and a sad memory of the Ball dance for Grizabella, while lighting the jazz-classic fireworks for Mr. Mistoffelees; indeed, trying to do justice to the variety of T. S. Eliot's characters in as wide a span of dance styles has been a fascinating and frightening task—but with two such brilliant teams of performers and the joy of working again with our production team, one of the most exciting and rewarding I can remember.

# 'A giant playground for cats' Designed by John Napier

The Winter Garden Theatre has been substantially altered to create the setting for this production—'a giant playground for cats'. Immediately we enter, the set is all around us, stretching right past us up to the mezzanine. The designer, John Napier, has created a complete environmental space for the show, taking the audience 'into a world which uses real objects to conjure up fantasy, that they may at first find slightly disorienting and perhaps make them wonder what is going to happen and how'.

When first discussing ways of staging *Cats* the production team felt that one important prerequisite was that they needed a theatre 'where it would be possible to charge the atmosphere even before the performance begins' and that this would not be possible in a theatre with a traditional proscenium arch stage. In London, they rediscovered the New London Theatre with its revolving stage and flexible seating. For the production in New York, however, the Winter Garden Theatre was selected for its huge open spaces, which would offer a similar flexibility (in spite of its proscenium) and an even more intense theatricality (because of it). In devising a visual image for the show—the leap in the dark from script to stage—John Napier wanted to create 'a world for *Cats* that would not only achieve a greater degree of intimacy with the audience than is possible in most conventional theatres but would also point up the humour of the show and its occasional whackiness'. At the Winter Garden, he has been able to use the whole theatre by giving the stage fingers stretching out into the audience, making hidden holes for surprise entrances and exits and even relocating some of the seats. Most members of the audience will find themselves, surprisingly, almost irresistibly close to the performing area.

He started work on the designs in November 1980, and began trying to visualise a place where cats might congregate together, bearing in mind that he also had to incorporate maximum room for dancing. Everything in the resulting playground cum rubbish dump was constructed to a cat's scale—three and a bit times life size—huge garbage cans, an abandoned car, massive tires, bicycles, even used tubes of toothpaste, worn-out Christmas decorations and lots of garbage from which the cats can improvise various disguises enabling them to tell the story from the objects they find lying around. John Napier and his team spent the entire summer of 1982 first dismantling large sections of the auditorium, redesigning other sections and then starting to rebuild bit by bit. In most productions, the designer and his team can usually go out and buy the necessary props or improvise them in some way but in *Cats* although the set is made up of items we chuck out every day most have had to be specifically made to scale.

When creating the costumes and make-up for each character John Napier has followed the hints of T. S. Eliot's text, blending together the cat and human elements. The costumes are, in addition, naturally very flexible and easy to move in—an essential feature in a show which contains such an important dance element.

JOHN NAPIER'S MODEL OF THE SET FOR THE AMERICAN PRODUCTION

14

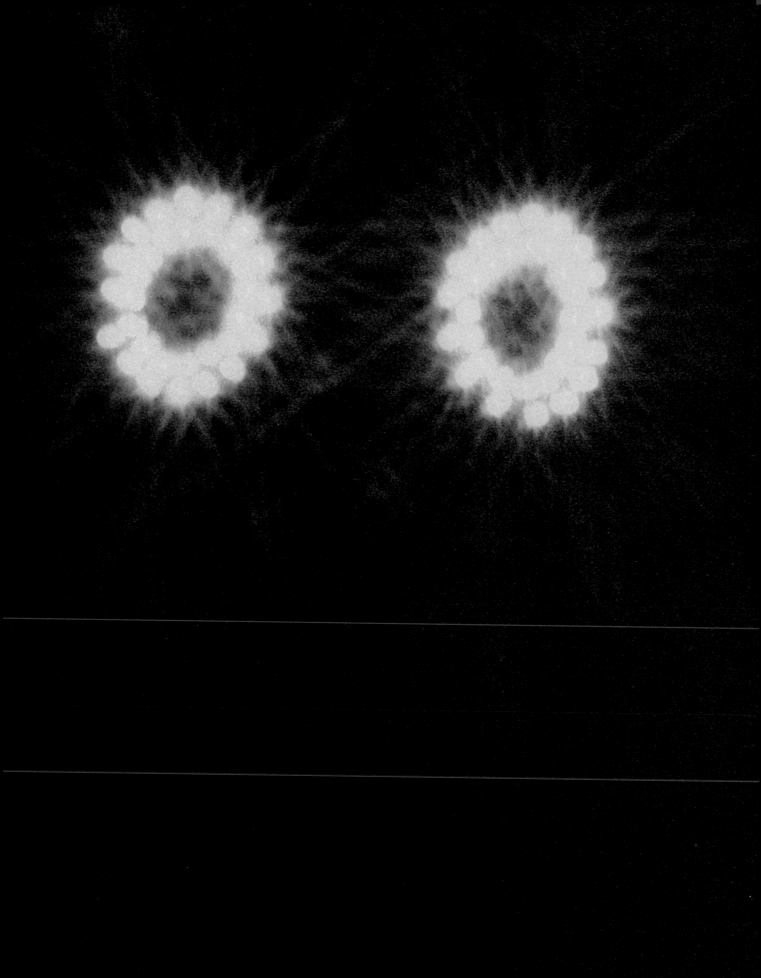

## from Jellicle Songs for Jellicle Cats

Are you blind when you're born? Can you see in the dark?
Can you look at a king? Would you sit on his throne?
Can you say of your bite that it's worse than your bark?
Are you cock of the walk when you're walking alone?
When you fall on your head do you land on your feet?
Are you tense when you sense there's a storm in the air?
Can you find your way back when you're lost in the street?
Do you know how to go to the Heaviside Layer?

Can you ride on a broomstick to places far distant
Familiar with candle, with book and with bell?
Were you Whittington's friend? the Pied Piper's assistant?
Have you been an alumnus of heaven or hell?
Are you mean like a minx? are you lean like a lynx?
Are you keen to be seen when you're smelling a rat?
Were you there when the pharaohs commissioned the sphinx?
If you were, and you are, you're a Jellicle cat.

We can dive through the air like a flying trapeze
We can turn double somersaults, bounce on a tyre,
We can run up a wall, we can swing through the trees,
We can balance on bars, we can walk on a wire.

Can you sing at the same time, in more than one key
Duets by Rossini and waltzes by Strauss?
And can you (as cats do) begin with a 'C'
That always triumphantly brings down the house?

Jellicle cats are queen-of-the-nights
Singing at astronomical heights
Handelling pieces from the Messiah
Hallelujah, angelical choir

The mystical divinity of unashamed felinity
Round the cathedral rang *Vivat!*
Life to the everlasting cat
Feline, fearless, faithful and true
To others who do what Jellicles do and Jellicles can

There's a man over there with a look of surprise,
As much as to say, Well now how about that?
Do I actually see with my own very eyes
A man who's not heard of a Jellicle cat?

# The Naming of Cats

The Naming of Cats is a difficult matter,
    It isn't just one of your holiday games;
You may think at first I'm as mad as a hatter
When I tell you, a cat must have THREE DIFFERENT
        NAMES.
First of all, there's the name that the family use daily,
    Such as Peter, Augustus, Alonzo or James,
Such as Victor or Jonathan, George or Bill Bailey—
    All of them sensible everyday names.
There are fancier names if you think they sound sweeter,
    Some for the gentlemen, some for the dames:
Such as Plato, Admetus, Electra, Demeter—
    But all of them sensible everyday names.
But I tell you, a cat needs a name that's particular,
    A name that's peculiar, and more dignified,
Else how can he keep up his tail perpendicular,
    Or spread out his whiskers, or cherish his pride?
Of names of this kind, I can give you a quorum,
    Such as Munkustrap, Quaxo, or Coricopat,
Such as Bombalurina, or else Jellylorum—
    Names that never belong to more than one cat.
But above and beyond there's still one name left over,
    And that is the name that you never will guess;
The name that no human research can discover—
    But THE CAT HIMSELF KNOWS, and will never confess.
When you notice a cat in profound meditation,
    The reason, I tell you, is always the same:
His mind is engaged in a rapt contemplation
    Of the thought, of the thought, of the thought of his name:
        His ineffable effable
        Effanineffable
Deep and inscrutable singular Name.

THE OLD GUMBIE CAT                                    CATS JJ. 81.

# The Old Gumbie Cat

I have a Gumbie Cat in mind, her name is Jennyanydots;
Her coat is of the tabby kind, with tiger stripes and leopard spots.
All day she sits upon the stair or on the steps or on the mat:
She sits and sits and sits and sits—and that's what makes a
     Gumbie Cat!

But when the day's hustle and bustle is done,
Then the Gumbie Cat's work is but hardly begun.
And when all the family's is bed and asleep,
She tucks up her skirts to the basement to creep.
She is deeply concerned with the ways of the mice—
Their behaviour's not good and their manners not nice;
So when she has got them lined up on the matting,
She teaches them music, crocheting and tatting.

I have a Gumbie Cat in mind, her name is Jennyanydots;
Her equal would be hard to find, she likes the warm and sunny spots.
All day she sits beside the hearth or in the sun or on my hat:
She sits and sits and sits and sits—and that's what makes a
    Gumbie Cat!

But when the day's hustle and bustle is done,
Then the Gumbie Cat's work is but hardly begun.
As she finds that the mice will not ever keep quiet,
She is sure it is due to irregular diet
And believing that nothing is done without trying,
She sets right to work with her baking and frying.
She makes them a mouse-cake of bread and dried peas,
And a *beautiful* fry of lean bacon and cheese.

I have a Gumbie Cat in mind, her name is Jennyanydots;
The curtain-cord she likes to wind, and tie it into sailor-knots.
She sits upon the window-sill, or anything that's smooth and flat:
She sits and sits and sits and sits—and that's what makes a
      Gumbie Cat!

    But when the day's hustle and bustle is done,
    Then the Gumbie Cat's work is but hardly begun.
    She thinks that the cockroaches just need employment
    To prevent them from idle and wanton destroyment.
    So she's formed, from that lot of disorderly louts,
    A troop of well-disciplined helpful boy-scouts,
    With a purpose in life and a good deed to do—
    And she's even created a Beetles' Tattoo.

So for Old Gumbie Cats let us now give three cheers—
On whom well-ordered households depend, it appears.

JENNYANYDOTS WITH THE BEETLES TATTOO

THE RUM TUM TUGGER.

JC CATS 81.

## The Rum Tum Tugger

The Rum Tum Tugger is a Curious Cat:
If you offer him pheasant he would rather have grouse.
If you put him in a house he would much prefer a flat,
If you put him in a flat then he'd rather have a house.
If you set him on a mouse then he only wants a rat,
If you set him on a rat then he'd rather chase a mouse.
Yes the Rum Tum Tugger is a Curious Cat—
    And there isn't any call for me to shout it:
        For he will do
        As he do do
            And there's no doing anything about it!

THE RUM TUM TUGGER AND BOMBALURINA

The Rum Tum Tugger is a terrible bore:
When you let him in, then he wants to be out;
He's always on the wrong side of every door,
And as soon as he's at home, then he'd like to get about.
He likes to lie in the bureau drawer,
But he makes such a fuss if he can't get out.
Yes the Rum Tum Tugger is a Curious Cat—
    And it isn't any use for you to doubt it:
        For he will do
        As he do do
            And there's no doing anything about it!

The Rum Tum Tugger is a curious beast:
His disobliging ways are a matter of habit.
If you offer him fish then he always wants a feast;
When there isn't any fish then he won't eat rabbit.
If you offer him cream then he sniffs and sneers,
For he only likes what he finds for himself;
So you'll catch him in it right up to the ears,
If you put it away on the larder shelf.
The Rum Tum Tugger is artful and knowing,
The Rum Tum Tugger doesn't care for a cuddle;
But he'll leap on your lap in the middle of your sewing,
For there's nothing he enjoys like a horrible muddle.
Yes the Rum Tum Tugger is a Curious Cat—
    And there isn't any need for me to spout it:
       For he will do
       As he do do
         And there's no doing anything about it!

GRIZABELLA          OATS JN. 81.

## Grizabella: the Glamour Cat

She haunted many a low resort
Near the grimy road of Tottenham Court;
She flitted about the No Man's Land
From The Rising Sun to The Friend at Hand.
And the postman sighed, as he scratched his head:
"You'd really ha' thought she'd ought to be dead
And who would ever suppose that *that*
Was Grizabella, the Glamour Cat!"

BUSTOPHER JONES  CATS JO 81

## Bustopher Jones: the Cat About Town

Bustopher Jones is *not* skin and bones—
In fact, he's remarkably fat.
He doesn't haunt pubs—he has eight or nine clubs,
For he's the St. James's Street Cat!
He's the Cat we all greet as he walks down the street
In his coat of fastidious black:
No commonplace mousers have such well-cut trousers
Or such an impeccable back.
In the whole of St. James's the smartest of names is
The name of this Brummell of Cats;
And we're all of us proud to be nodded or bowed to
By Bustopher Jones in white spats!

His visits are occasional to the *Senior Educational*
And it is against the rules
For any one Cat to belong both to that
And the *Joint Superior Schools.*
For a similar reason, when game is in season
He is found, not at *Fox's*, but *Blimp's;*
He is frequently seen at the gay *Stage and Screen*
Which is famous for winkles and shrimps.
In the season of venison he gives his ben'son
To the *Pothunter's* succulent bones;
And just before noon's not a moment too soon
To drop in for a drink at the *Drones.*
When he's seen in a hurry there's probably curry
At the *Siamese*—or at the *Glutton;*
If he looks full of gloom then he's lunched at the *Tomb*
On cabbage, rice pudding and mutton.

So, much in this way, passes Bustopher's day—
At one club or another he's found.
It can be no surprise that under our eyes
He has grown unmistakably round.
He's a twenty-five pounder, or I am a bounder,
And he's putting on weight every day:
But he's so well preserved because he's observed
All his life a routine, so he'll say.
Or, to put it in rhyme: 'I shall last out my time'
Is the word of this stoutest of Cats.
It must and it shall be Spring in Pall Mall
While Bustopher Jones wears white spats!

BUSTOPHER WITH CARBUCKETY AND POUNCIVAL

## Mungojerrie and Rumpelteazer

Mungojerrie and Rumpelteazer were a very
    notorious couple of cats.
As knockabout clowns, quick-change comedians,
    tight-rope walkers and acrobats
They had an extensive reputation. They made
    their home in Victoria Grove—
That was merely their centre of operation, for
    they were incurably given to rove.
They were very well known in Cornwall Gardens,
    in Launceston Place and in Kensington Square—
They had really a little more reputation than a
    couple of cats can very well bear.

If the area window was found ajar
And the basement looked like a field of war,
If a tile or two came loose on the roof,
Which presently ceased to be waterproof,
If the drawers were pulled out from the bedroom chests,
And you couldn't find one of your winter vests,
Or after supper one of the girls
Suddenly missed her Woolworth pearls:
Then the family would say: 'It's that horrible cat!
It was Mungojerrie—or Rumpelteazer!'—And most of the
      time they left it at that.

Mungojerrie and Rumpelteazer had a very unusual gift of the
      gab.
They were highly efficient cat-burglars as well, and remarkably
      smart at a smash-and-grab.
They made their home in Victoria Grove. They had no
      regular occupation.
They were plausible fellows, and liked to engage a friendly
      policeman in conversation.

When the family assembled for Sunday dinner,
With their minds made up that they wouldn't get thinner
On Argentine joint, potatoes and greens,
And the cook would appear from behind the scenes
And say in a voice that was broken with sorrow:
'I'm afraid you must wait and have dinner *tomorrow!*
For the joint has gone from the oven—like that!'
Then the family would say: 'It's that horrible cat!
It was Mungojerrie—or Rumpelteazer!'—And most of the
      time they left it at that.

Mungojerrie and Rumpelteazer had a wonderful way of
      working together.
And some of the time you would say it was luck, and some of
      the time you would say it was weather.
They would go through the house like a hurricane, and no
      sober person could take his oath
Was it Mungojerrie—or Rumpelteazer? or could you have
      sworn that it mightn't be both?

And when you heard a dining-room smash
Or up from the pantry there came a loud crash
Or down from the library came a loud *ping*
From a vase which was commonly said to be Ming—
Then the family would say: 'Now which was which cat?
It was Mungojerrie! AND Rumpelteazer!'—And there's
      nothing at all to be done about that!

# Old Deuteronomy

Old Deuteronomy's lived a long time;
   He's a Cat who has lived many lives in succession.
He was famous in proverb and famous in rhyme
   A long while before Queen Victoria's accession.
Old Deuteronomy's buried nine wives
   And more—I am tempted to say, ninety-nine;
And his numerous progeny prospers and thrives
   And the village is proud of him in his decline.
At the sight of that placid and bland physiognomy,
   When he sits in the sun on the vicarage wall,
The Oldest Inhabitant croaks: 'Well, of all . . .
   Things . . . Can it be . . . really! . . . No! . . . Yes! . . .
      Ho! hi!
      Oh, my eye!
My mind may be wandering, but I confess
I *believe* it is Old Deuteronomy!'

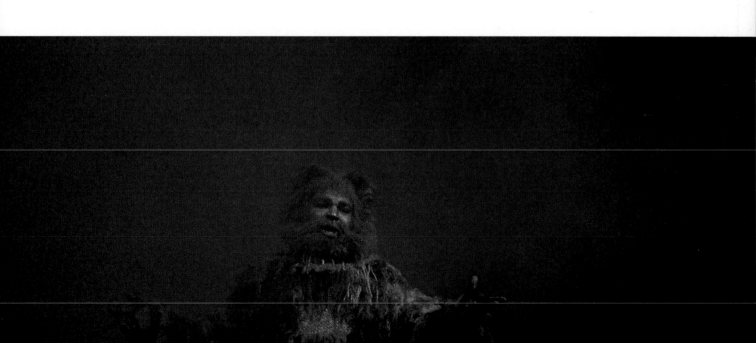

Old Deuteronomy sits in the street,
　　He sits in the High Street on market day;
The bullocks may bellow, the sheep they may bleat,
　　But the dogs and the herdsmen will turn them away.
The cars and the lorries run over the kerb,
　　And the villagers put up a notice: ROAD CLOSED—
So that nothing untoward may chance to disturb
　　Deuteronomy's rest when he feels so disposed
Or when he's engaged in domestic economy:
　　And the Oldest Inhabitant croaks: 'Well, of all . . .
　　Things . . . Can it be . . . really! . . . No! . . . Yes! . . .
　　　　Ho! hi!
　　　　Oh, my eye!
My sight's unreliable, but I can guess
That the cause of the trouble is Old Deuteronomy!

Old Deuteronomy lies on the floor
　　Of the Fox and French Horn for his afternoon sleep;
And when the men say: 'There's just time for one more,'
　　Then the landlady from her back parlour will peep
And say: 'Now then, out you go, by the back door,
　　For Old Deuteronomy mustn't be woken—
I'll have the police if there's any uproar'—
　　And out they all shuffle, without a word spoken.
The digestive repose of that feline's gastronomy
　　Must never be broken, whatever befall:
And the Oldest Inhabitant croaks: 'Well, of all . . .
　　Things . . . Can it be . . . really! . . . Yes! . . . No! . . .
　　　　Ho! hi!
　　　　Oh, my eye!
My legs may be tottery, I must go slow
And be careful of Old Deuteronomy!'

2.

OLD DEUTERONOMY

CATS. JN 81

8
DOGS

CATS JN 81.

# The Battle of the Pekes and the Pollicles

The Pekes and the Pollicles, everyone knows,
Are proud and implacable passionate foes;
It is always the same, wherever one goes.
And the Pugs and the Poms, although most people say
That they do not like fighting, yet once in a way,
They will now and again join in to the fray
And they
   Bark bark bark bark
   Bark bark BARK BARK
  Until you can hear them all over the Park.


Now on the occasion of which I shall speak
Almost nothing had happened for nearly a week
(And that's a long time for a Pol or a Peke).
The big Police Dog was away from his beat—
I don't know the reason, but most people think
He'd slipped into the Wellington Arms for a drink—
And no one at all was about on the street
When a Peke and a Pollicle happened to meet.
They did not advance, or exactly retreat,
But they glared at each other, and scraped their hind
 feet,
And started to
   Bark bark bark bark
   Bark bark BARK BARK
  Until you could hear them all over the Park.


Now the Peke, although people may say what they
 please,
Is no British Dog, but a Heathen Chinese.
And so all the Pekes, when they heard the uproar,
Some came to the window, some came to the door;
There were surely a dozen, more likely a score.
And together they started to grumble and wheeze
In their huffery-snuffery Heathen Chinese.
But a terrible din is what Pollicles like,
For your Pollicle Dog is a dour Yorkshire tyke,

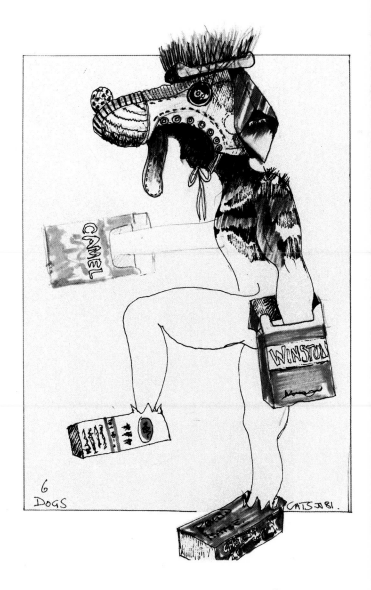

And his braw Scottish cousins are snappers and biters,
And every dog-jack of them notable fighters;
And so they stepped out, with their pipers in order,
Playing *When the Blue Bonnets Came Over the Border.*
Then the Pugs and the Poms held no longer aloof,
But some from the balcony, some from the roof,
Joined in
To the din
With a
          Bark bark bark bark
          Bark bark BARK BARK
Until you could hear them all over the Park.

## from the Marching Song of the Pollicle Dogs

*There are dogs out of every nation,*
*The Irish, the Welsh and the Dane;*
*The Russian, the Dutch, the Dalmatian,*
*And even from China and Spain;*
*The Poodle, the Pom, the Alsatian*
*And the mastiff who walks on a chain.*
*And to those that are frisky and frollical*
*Let my meaning be perfectly plain:*
*That my name it is Little Tom Pollicle—*
*And you'd better not do it again.*

Now when these bold heroes together assembled,
The traffic all stopped, and the Underground trembled,
And some of the neighbours were so much afraid
That they started to ring up the Fire Brigade.
When suddenly, up from a small basement flat,
Why who should stalk out but the GREAT RUMPUSCAT.
His eyes were like fireballs fearfully blazing,
He gave a great yawn, and his jaws were amazing;
And when he looked out through the bars of the area,
You never saw anything fiercer or hairier.
And what with the glare of his eyes and his yawning,
The Pekes and the Pollicles quickly took warning.
He looked at the sky and he gave a great leap—
And they every last one of them scattered like sheep.

*And when the Police Dog returned to his beat,*
*There wasn't a single one left in the street.*

THE GREAT RUMPUSCAT

## The Song of the Jellicles

*Jellicle Cats come out to-night,*
  *Jellicle Cats come one come all:*
*The Jellicle Moon is shining bright—*
  *Jellicles come to the Jellicle Ball.*

*Jellicle Cats are black and white,*
*Jellicle Cats are rather small;*
*Jellicle Cats are merry and bright,*
*And pleasant to hear when they caterwaul.*
*Jellicle Cats have cheerful faces,*
*Jellicle Cats have bright black eyes;*
*They like to practise their airs and graces*
*And wait for the Jellicle Moon to rise.*

*Jellicle Cats develop slowly,*
*Jellicle Cats are not too big;*
*Jellicle Cats are roly-poly,*
*They know how to dance a gavotte and a jig.*
*Until the Jellicle Moon appears*
*They make their toilette and take their repose*
*Jellicles wash behind their ears,*
*Jellicles dry between their toes.*

VICTORIA

*Jellicle Cats are white and black,*
*Jellicle Cats are of moderate size;*
*Jellicles jump like a jumping-jack,*
*Jellicle Cats have moonlit eyes.*
*They're quiet enough in the morning hours,*
*They're quiet enough in the afternoon,*
*Reserving their terpsichorean powers*
*To dance by the light of the Jellicle Moon.*

*Jellicle Cats are black and white,*
*Jellicle Cats (as I said) are small;*
*If it happens to be a stormy night*
*They will practise a caper or two in the hall.*
*If it happens the sun is shining bright*
*You would say they had nothing to do at all:*
*They are resting and saving themselves to be right*
*For the Jellicle Moon and the Jellicle Ball.*

←  JELLYLORUM

61

# from Gus: the Theatre Cat

GUS AND JELLYLORUM

Gus is the Cat at the Theatre Door.
His name, as I ought to have told you before,
Is really Asparagus. That's such a fuss
To pronounce, that we usually call him just Gus.
His coat's very shabby, he's thin as a rake,
And he suffers from palsy that makes his paw shake.
Yet he was, in his youth, quite the smartest of Cats—
But no longer a terror to mice and to rats.
For he isn't the Cat that he was in his prime;
Though his name was quite famous, he says, in its time.
And whenever he joins his friends at their club
(Which takes place at the back of the neighbouring pub)
He loves to regale them, if someone else pays,
With anecdotes drawn from his palmiest days.
For he once was a Star of the highest degree—
He has acted with Irving, he's acted with Tree.
And he likes to relate his success on the Halls,
Where the Gallery once gave him seven cat-calls.
But his grandest creation, as he loves to tell,
Was Firefrorefiddle, the Field of the Fell.

'I have played', so he says, 'every possible part,
And I used to know seventy speeches by heart.
I'd extemporize back-chat, I knew how to gag,
And I knew how to let the cat out of the bag.

Then, if someone will give him a toothful of gin,
He will tell how he once played a part in *East Lynne.*
At a Shakespeare performance he once walked on pat,
When some actor suggested the need for a cat.

And he says: 'Now, these kittens, they do not get trained
As we did in the days when Victoria reigned.
They never get drilled in a regular troupe,
And they think they are smart, just to jump through a hoop.'
And he'll say, as he scratches himself with his claws,
'Well, the Theatre's certainly not what it was.
These modern productions are all very well,
But there's nothing to equal, from what I hear tell,
   That moment of mystery
   When I made history
As Firefrorefiddle, the Fiend of the Fell.'

GROWLTIGER

CATS            JV 81.

## Growltiger's Last Stand

Growltiger was a Bravo Cat, who travelled on a barge:
In fact he was the roughest cat that ever roamed at large.
From Gravesend up to Oxford he pursued his evil aims,
Rejoicing in his title of 'The Terror of the Thames'.

His manners and appearance did not calculate to please;
His coat was torn and seedy, he was baggy at the knees;
One ear was somewhat missing, no need to tell you why,
And he scowled upon a hostile world from one forbidding eye.

The cottagers of Rotherhithe knew something of his fame;
At Hammersmith and Putney people shuddered at his name.
They would fortify the hen-house, lock up the silly goose,
When the rumour ran along the shore: GROWLTIGER'S ON THE LOOSE!

Woe to the weak canary, that fluttered from its cage;
Woe to the pampered Pekinese, that faced Growltiger's rage;
Woe to the bristly Bandicoot, that lurks on foreign ships,
And woe to any Cat with whom Growltiger came to grips!

But most to Cats of foreign race his hatred had been vowed;
To Cats of foreign name and race no quarter was allowed.
The Persian and the Siamese regarded him with fear—
Because it was a Siamese had mauled his missing ear.

Now on a peaceful summer night, all nature seemed at play,
The tender moon was shining bright, the barge at Molesey lay.
All in the balmy moonlight it lay rocking on the tide—
And Growltiger was disposed to show his sentimental side.

His bucko mate, GRUMBUSKIN, long since had disappeared,
For to the Bell at Hampton he had gone to wet his beard;
And his bosun, TUMBLEBRUTUS, he too had stol'n away—
In the yard behind the Lion he was prowling for his prey.

In the forepeak of the vessel Growltiger sate alone,
Concentrating his attention on the Lady GRIDDLEBONE.
And his raffish crew were sleeping in their barrels and their
    bunks—
As the Siamese came creeping in their sampans and their junks.

◄—GROWLTIGER AND GRIDDLEBONE

Growltiger had no eye or ear for aught but Griddlebone,
And the Lady seemed enraptured by his manly baritone,
Disposed to relaxation, and awaiting no surprise—
But the moonlight shone reflected from a thousand bright blue
    eyes.

And closer still and closer the sampans circled round,
And yet from all the enemy there was not heard a sound.
The lovers sang their last duet, in danger of their lives—
For the foe was armed with toasting forks and cruel carving
    knives.

Then GILBERT gave the signal to his fierce Mongolian horde;
With a frightful burst of fireworks the Chinks they swarmed aboard.
Abandoning their sampans, and their pullaways and junks,
They battened down the hatches on the crew within their bunks.

Then Griddlebone she gave a screech, for she was badly skeered;
I am sorry to admit it, but she quickly disappeared.
She probably escaped with ease, I'm sure she was not drowned—
But a serried ring of flashing steel Growltiger did surround.

THE SIAMESE →

The ruthless foe pressed forward, in stubborn rank on rank;
Growltiger to his vast surprise was forced to walk the plank.
He who a hundred victims had driven to that drop,
At the end of all his crimes was forced to go ker-flip, ker-flop.

Oh there was joy in Wapping when the news flew through the land;
At Maidenhead and Henley there was dancing on the strand.
Rats were roasted whole at Brentford, and at Victoria Dock,
And a day of celebration was commanded in Bangkok.

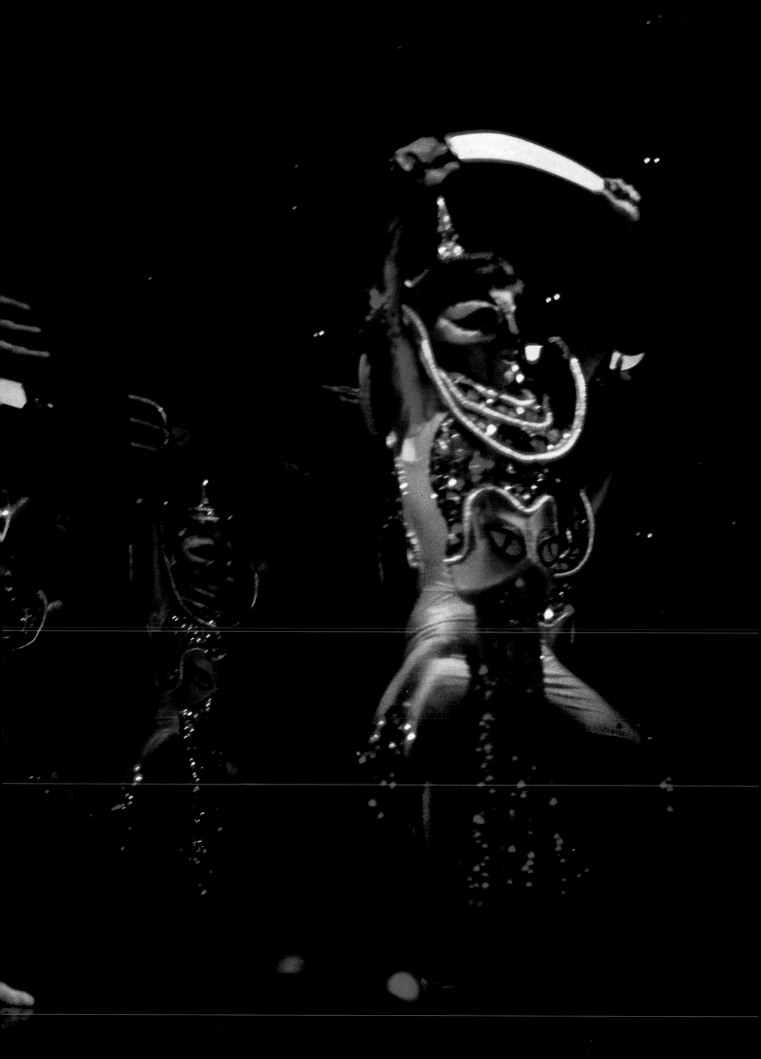

# from Skimbleshanks: the Railway Cat

There's a whisper down the line at 11.39
When the Night Mail's ready to depart,
Saying 'Skimble where is Skimble has he gone to hunt the thimble?
We must find him or the train can't start.'
All the guards and all the porters and the stationmaster's daughters
They are searching high and low,
Saying 'Skimble where is Skimble for unless he's very nimble
Then the Night Mail just can't go.'
At 11.42 then the signal's overdue
And the passengers are frantic to a man—
Then Skimble will appear and he'll saunter to the rear:
He's been busy in the luggage van!
    He gives one flash of his glass-green eyes
        And the signal goes 'All Clear!'
    And we're off at last for the northern part
        Of the Northern Hemisphere!

← SKIMBLESHANKS WITH TUMBLEBRUTUS AND BOMBALURINA

You may say that by and large it is Skimble who's in charge
Of the Sleeping Car Express.
From the driver and the guards to the bagmen playing cards
He will supervise them all, more or less.
Down the corridor he paces and examines all the faces
Of the travellers in the First and in the Third;
He establishes control by a regular patrol
And he'd know at once if anything occurred.

He will watch you without winking and he sees what you are thinking
And it's certain that he doesn't approve
Of hilarity and riot, so the folk are very quiet
When Skimble is about and on the move.
   You can play no pranks with Skimbleshanks!
     He's a Cat that cannot be ignored;
   So nothing goes wrong on the Northern Mail
     When Skimbleshanks is aboard.

# Macavity: the Mystery Cat

Macavity's a Mystery Cat: he's called the Hidden Paw—
For he's the master criminal who can defy the Law.
He's the bafflement of Scotland Yard, the Flying Squad's despair:
For when they reach the scene of crime—*Macavity's not there!*

Macavity, Macavity, there's no one like Macavity,
He's broken every human law, he breaks the law of gravity.
His powers of levitation would make a fakir stare,
And when you reach the scene of crime—*Macavity's not there!*
You may seek him in the basement, you may look up in the air—
But I tell you once and once again, *Macavity's not there!*

Macavity's a ginger cat, he's very tall and thin;
You would know him if you saw him, for his eyes are sunken in.
His brow is deeply lined with thought, his head is highly domed;
His coat is dusty from neglect, his whiskers are uncombed.
He sways his head from side to side, with movements like a snake;
And when you think he's half asleep, he's always wide awake.

Macavity, Macavity, there's no one like Macavity,
For he's a fiend in feline shape, a monster of depravity.
You may meet him in a by-street, you may see him in the square—
But when a crime's discovered, then *Macavity's not there!*

He's outwardly respectable. (They say he cheats at cards.)
And his footprints are not found in any file of Scotland Yard's.
And when the larder's looted, or the jewel-case is rifled,
Or when the milk is missing, or another Peke's been stifled,
Or the greenhouse glass is broken, and the trellis past repair—
Ay, there's the wonder of the thing! *Macavity's not there!*

DEMETER

And when the Foreign Office find a Treaty's gone astray,
Or the Admiralty lose some plans and drawings by the way,
There may be a scrap of paper in the hall or on the stair—
But it's useless to investigate—*Macavity's not there!*
And when the loss has been disclosed, the Secret Service say:
'It *must* have been Macavity!'—but he's a mile away.
You'll be sure to find him resting, or a-licking of his thumbs,
Or engaged in doing complicated long division sums.

Macavity, Macavity, there's no one like Macavity,
There never was a Cat of such deceitfulness and suavity.
He always has an alibi, and one or two to spare:
At whatever time the deed took place—MACAVITY WASN'T THERE!
And they say that all the Cats whose wicked deeds are widely known
(I might mention Mungojerrie, I might mention Griddlebone)
Are nothing more than agents for the Cat who all the time
Just controls their operations: the Napoleon of Crime!

← MACAVITY

BOMBALURINA AND DEMETER

MACAVITY'S NOT THERE!

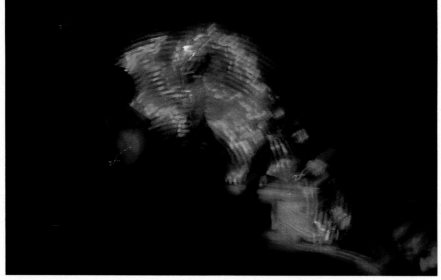

MR. MISTOFFELEES                                    CATS JV 81.

# Mr. Mistoffelees

You ought to know Mr. Mistoffelees!
The Original Conjuring Cat—
(There can be no doubt about that).
Please listen to me and don't scoff. All his
Inventions are off his own bat.
There's no such Cat in the metropolis;
He holds all the patent monopolies
For performing surprising illusions
And creating eccentric confusions.
    At prestidigitation
      And at legerdemain
    He'll defy examination
      And deceive you again.
The greatest magicians have something to learn
From Mr. Mistoffelees' Conjuring Turn.
Presto!
    Away we go!
      And we all say: OH!
        Well I never!
        Was there ever
        A Cat so clever
          As Magical Mr. Mistoffelees!

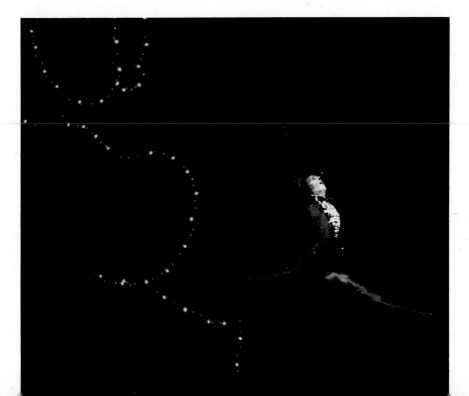

MAGICAL MR. MISTOFFELEES

92

He is quiet and small, he is black
From his ears to the tip of his tail;
He can creep through the tiniest crack,
He can walk on the narrowest rail.

He can pick any card from a pack,
He is equally cunning with dice;
He is always deceiving you into believing
That he's only hunting for mice.
   He can play any trick with a cork
     Or a spoon and a bit of fish-paste;
  If you look for a knife or a fork
    And you think it is merely misplaced—
You have seen it one moment, and then it is *gawn!*
But you'll find it next week lying out on the lawn.
   And we all say: OH!
    Well I never!
    Was there ever
    A Cat so clever
     As Magical Mr. Mistoffelees!

His manner is vague and aloof,
You would think there was nobody shyer—
But his voice has been heard on the roof
When he was curled up by the fire.
And he's sometimes been heard by the fire
When he was about on the roof—
(At least we all *heard* that somebody purred)
Which is incontestable proof
  Of his singular magical powers:
    And I have known the family to call
  Him in from the garden for hours,
    While he was asleep in the hall.

And not long ago this phenomenal Cat
Produced *seven kittens* right out of a hat!
   And we all said: OH!
    Well I never!
    Did you ever
    Know a Cat so clever
     As Magical Mr. Mistoffelees!

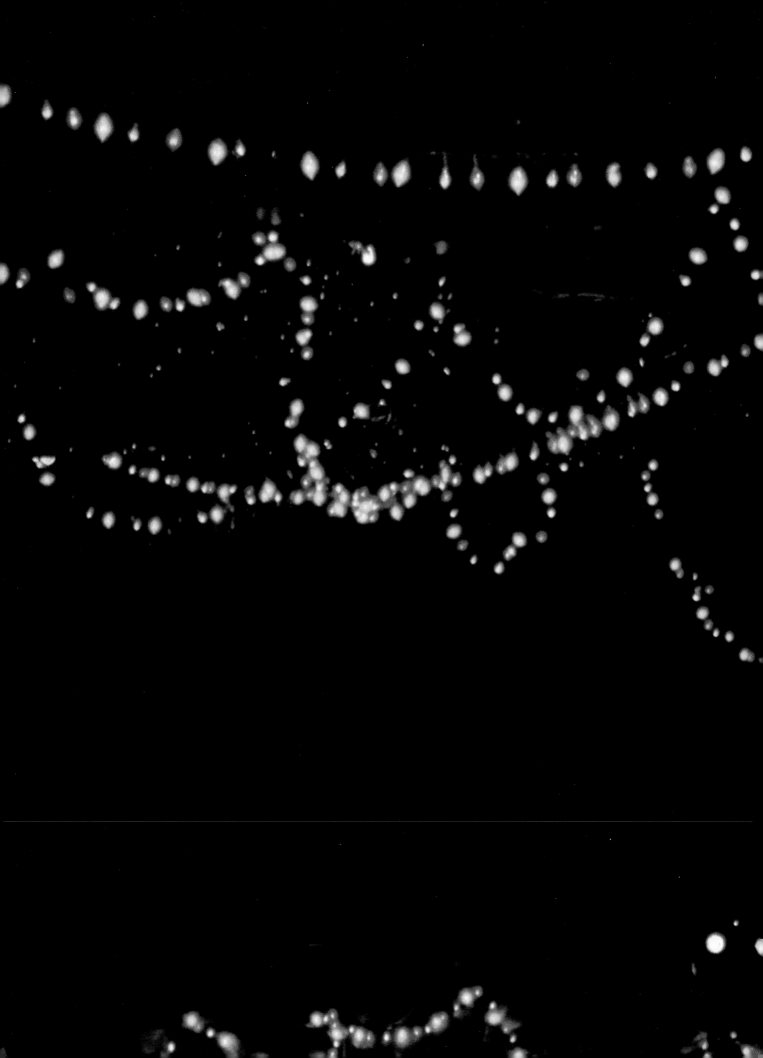

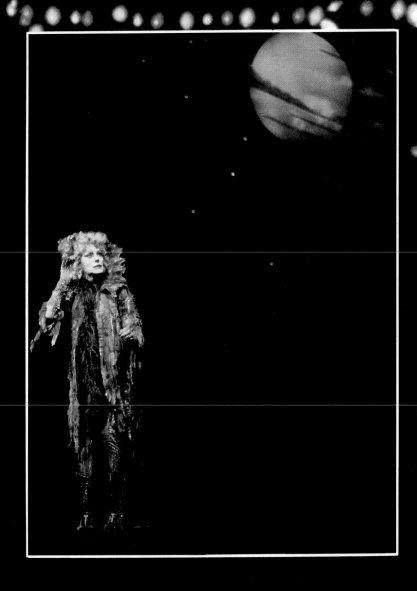

*Now Old Deuteronomy just before dawn*
*Through a silence you feel you could cut with a knife*
*Announces the cat who can now be reborn*
*And come back to a different Jellicle life.*

# Memory

Midnight, not a sound from the pavement.
Has the moon lost her memory?
She is smiling alone.
In the lamp light the withered leaves collect at my feet
And the wind begins to moan.

Memory. All alone in the moonlight
I can smile at the old days.
I was beautiful then.
I remember the time I knew what happiness was,
Let the memory live again.

Every street lamp seems to beat a fatalistic warning
Someone mutters and the street lamp gutters,
And soon it will be morning.

Daylight. I must wait for the sunrise
I must think of a new life
And I mustn't give in.
When the dawn comes tonight will be a memory, too
And a new day will begin.

Burnt-out ends of smoky days
The stale cold smell of morning.
The street lamp dies, another night is over,
Another day is dawning.

Touch me. It's so easy to leave me
All alone with the memory
Of my days in the sun.
If you touch me you'll understand what happiness is.
Look, a new day has begun.

## To the Heaviside Layer

Up up up past the Russell Hotel
Up up up to the Heaviside Layer

Up up up past the Russell Hotel
Up up up to the Heaviside Layer

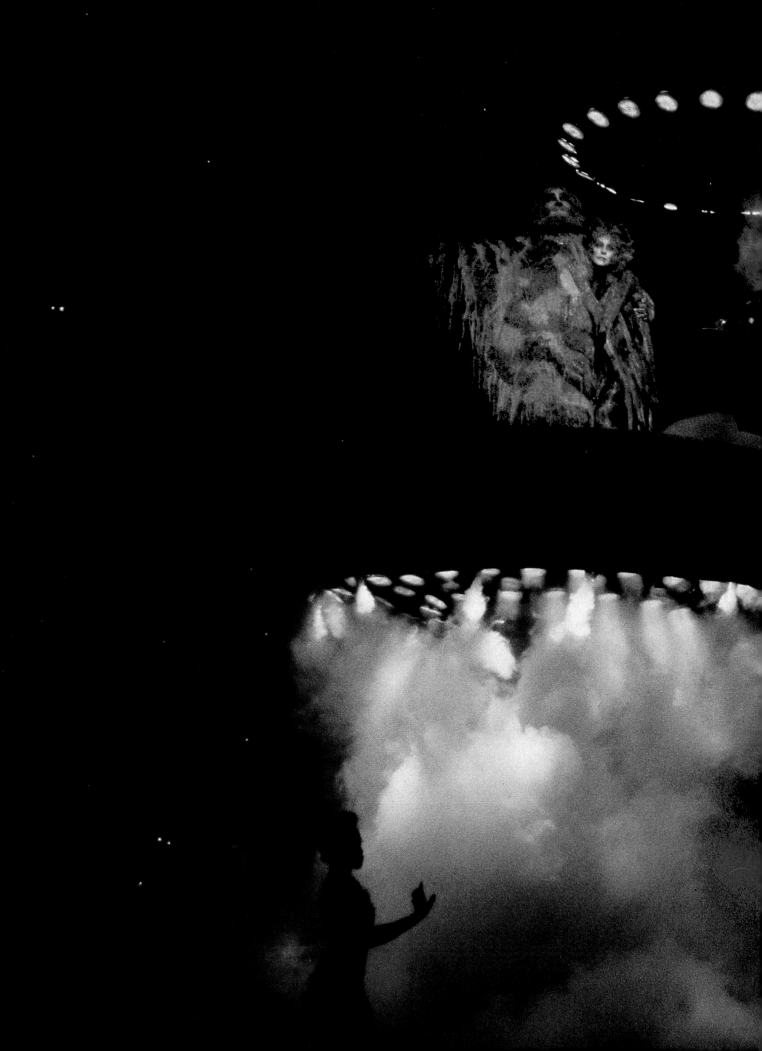

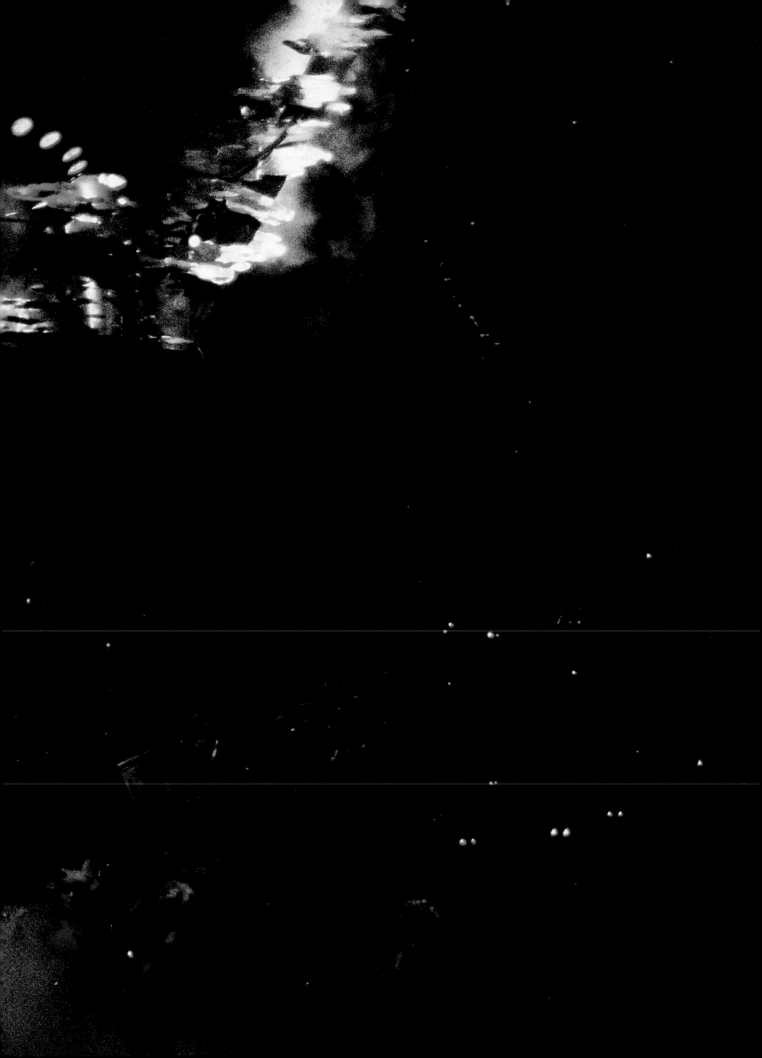

# The Ad-dressing of Cats

You've read of several kinds of Cat,
And my opinion now is that
You should need no interpreter
To understand their character.
You now have learned enough to see
That Cats are much like you and me
And other people whom we find
Possessed of various types of mind.
For some are sane and some are mad
And some are good and some are bad
And some are better, some are worse—
But all may be described in verse.
You've seen them both at work and games,
And learnt about their proper names,
Their habits and their habitat:
But
> How would you ad-dress a Cat?

So first, your memory I'll jog,
And say: A CAT IS NOT A DOG.

Now Dogs pretend they like to fight;
They often bark, more seldom bite;
But yet a Dog is, on the whole,
What you would call a simple soul.
Of course I'm not including Pekes,
And such fantastic canine freaks.

The usual Dog about the Town
Is much inclined to play the clown,
And far from showing too much pride
Is frequently undignified.
He's very easily taken in—
Just chuck him underneath the chin
Or slap his back or shake his paw,
And he will gambol and guffaw.
He's such an easy-going lout,
He'll answer any hail or shout.

Again I must remind you that
A Dog's a Dog—A CAT'S A CAT.

With Cats, some say, one rule is true:
*Don't speak till you are spoken to.*
Myself, I do not hold with that—
I say, you should ad-dress a Cat.
But always keep in mind that he
Resents familiarity.
I bow, and taking off my hat,
Ad-dress him in this form: O CAT!
But if he is the Cat next door,
Whom I have often met before
(He comes to see me in my flat)
I greet him with an OOPSA CAT!
I think I've heard them call him James—
But we've not got so far as names.

Before a Cat will condescend
To treat you as a trusted friend,
Some little token of esteem
Is needed, like a dish of cream;
And you might now and then supply
Some caviare, or Strassburg Pie,
Some potted grouse, or salmon paste—
He's sure to have his personal taste.
(I know a Cat, who makes a habit
Of eating nothing else but rabbit,
And when he's finished, licks his paws
So's not to waste the onion sauce.)
A Cat's entitled to expect
These evidences of respect.
And so in time you reach your aim,
And finally call him by his NAME.

So this is this, and that is that:
And there's how you AD-DRESS A CAT.

# from Jellicle Songs for Jellicle Cats

Practical cats, dramatical cats,
Pragmatical cats, fanatical cats,
Oratorical cats, delphicoracle cats,
Sceptical cats, dispeptical cats

Romantical cats, pedantical cats,
Critical cats, parasitical cats,
Allegorical cats, metaphorical cats,
Statistical cats and mystical cats,
Political cats, hypocritical cats,
Clerical cats, hysterical cats,
Cynical cats, rabbinical cats

Jellicle songs for Jellicle cats
Jellicle bells that Jellicles ring
Jellicle sharps and Jellicle flats
Jellicle songs that Jellicles sing

Jellicle songs for Jellicle cats
Jellicle songs for Jellicle cats
Jellicle songs for Jellicle cats
Jellicle songs for Jellicle cats

*Pollicle dogs and cats all must*
*Jellicle cats and dogs all must*
*Like undertakers, come to dust.*

**MUSIC BY ANDREW LLOYD WEBBER**  **BASED ON**
**"OLD POSSUM'S BOOK OF PRACTICAL CATS" BY**
**T. S. ELIOT**

Presented by Cameron Mackintosh, The Really Useful Company Limited, David Geffen and The Shubert Organization

### CAST
*(in amphibolical order)*

| | |
|---|---|
| Alonzo | Hector Jaime Mercado |
| Bustopher Jones/Asparagus/Growltiger | Stephen Hanan |
| Bombalurina | Donna King |
| Carbuckety | Steven Gelfer |
| Cassandra | René Ceballos |
| Coricopat/Mungojerrie | René Clemente |
| Demeter | Wendy Edmead |
| Etcetera/Rumpelteazer | Christine Langner |
| Grizabella | Betty Buckley |
| Jellylorum/Griddlebone | Bonnie Simmons |
| Jennyanydots | Anna McNeely |
| Mistoffelees | Timothy Scott |
| Munkustrap | Harry Groener |
| Old Deuteronomy | Ken Page |
| Plato/Macavity/Rumpuscat | Kenneth Ard |
| Pouncival | Herman W. Sebek |
| Rum Tum Tugger | Terrence V. Mann |
| Sillabub | Whitney Kershaw |
| Skimbleshanks | Reed Jones |
| Tantomile | Janet L. Hubert |
| Tumblebrutus | Robert Hoshour |
| Victoria | Cynthia Onrubia |
| The Cats Chorus | Walter Charles, Susan Powers, Carol Richards, Joel Robertson |

Executive Producers, R. Tyler Gatchell, Jr., Peter Neufeld; Orchestrations by David Cullen and Andrew Lloyd Webber; Production Musical Director, Stanley Lebowsky; Musical Director, Rene Wiegert; Sound by **Martin Levan;** Lighting Design by **David Hersey;** Designed by **John Napier;** Associate Director and Choreographer, **Gillian Lynne;** Directed by **Trevor Nunn.**

First American Performance at the Winter Garden Theatre October 7, 1982